I0797354

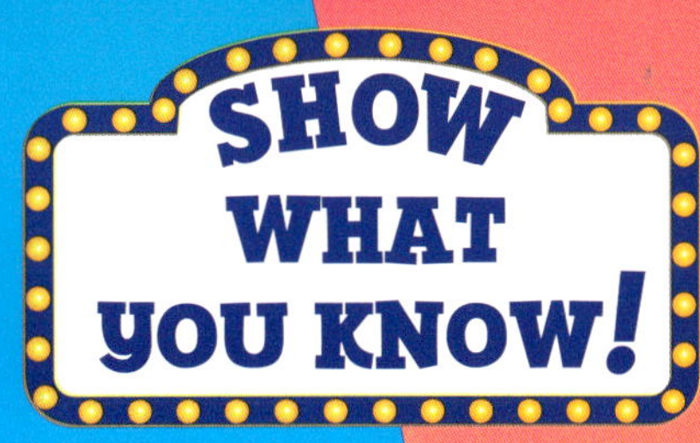

Finding the Right Research Topic

by Kelly Coleman

Go to
www.openlightbox.com
and enter this book's
unique code.

ACCESS CODE

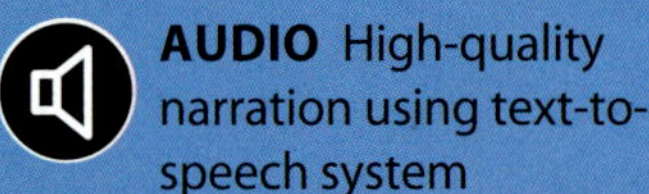

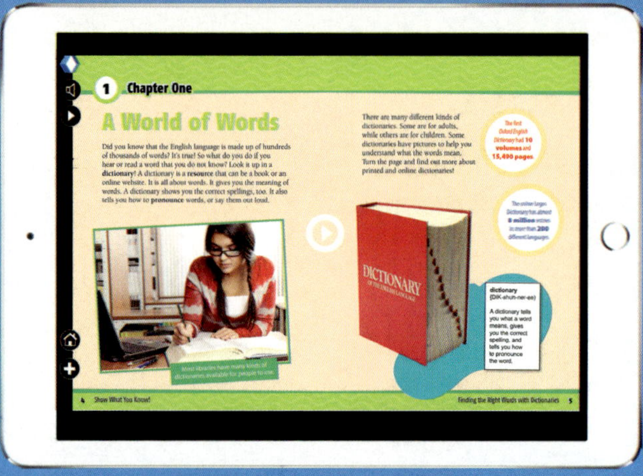

Lightbox is an all-inclusive digital solution for the teaching and learning of curriculum topics in an original, groundbreaking way. Lightbox is based on National Curriculum Standards.

STANDARD FEATURES OF LIGHTBOX

AUDIO High-quality narration using text-to-speech system

ACTIVITIES Printable PDFs that can be emailed and graded

SLIDESHOWS Pictorial overviews of key concepts

VIDEOS Embedded high-definition video clips

WEBLINKS Curated links to external, child-safe resources

TRANSPARENCIES Step-by-step layering of maps, diagrams, charts, and timelines

INTERACTIVE MAPS Interactive maps and aerial satellite imagery

QUIZZES Ten multiple choice questions that are automatically graded and emailed for teacher assessment

KEY WORDS Matching key concepts to their definitions

Finding the Right Research Topic

1 Chapter One

What Is Research?

Have you ever wondered, "Why is the sky blue?" Maybe you have watched a cartoon and asked, "Why do cats chase mice?" Or perhaps you have noticed trash on the side of the road. Did you think, "Where does this trash come from?" If you have ever asked a question and then worked to find the answer, you have done research. Research is a process to answer questions about a certain topic.

A research topic is the subject a person wants to learn about. For example, Ms. Patel asked her students to research questions about fish for a class project. There is a lot of information to learn about fish. Entire books have been written about them! Ms. Patel's students have to narrow this general topic down to a more specific topic for their projects. This topic should be turned into a question.

Ms. Patel's students have a lot of ideas for their projects.

Each student thinks about what he or she most wants to learn about fish. To help them, Ms. Patel asks, "What would you ask an expert about fish?"

Susie asks, "Why do humans need fish?"

Jack wonders, "What is the best way to catch a fish in Lake Michigan?"

Martina wants to know, "Why are fish in oceans different from fish in lakes?"

The science agency **NOAA** has been researching fish since **1970**.

More than **90 percent** of students use the **internet** for schoolwork and research.

Once the students have each chosen a topic and written a question, they can begin their research. They find **resources**. They read and take notes. In the end, they combine everything they learned into a paper, presentation, or other project. Research is exciting. But there are so many interesting topics to wonder about. In this book, you will learn some **strategies** to help you choose a research topic.

Books are one type of resource you might use in a research project.

Try This

Let's practice forming questions about different topics. Copy the chart below onto a separate sheet of paper. Leave some spaces between each topic. Under "Questions," list some questions you might ask about each topic.

Topic	Questions
Soccer	
China	
Water pollution	
Abraham Lincoln	

History of Research

3000 BC A temple in modern-day Iraq becomes one of the first libraries.

859 AD The University of Kaureein opens in Morocco. It is the oldest university to still exist.

Late 1500s According to legend, Galileo conducts an experiment to test gravity. He drops two balls from the Leaning Tower of Pisa to see if they land at the same time.

1752 Benjamin Franklin conducts his famous kite-flying experiment to answer research questions about lightning and electricity.

1768 The first edition of the *Encyclopædia Britannica* is published. It is the oldest encyclopedia in English.

1989 Computer scientist Tim Berners-Lee invents the World Wide Web, which becomes the internet.

2017 NASA announces updates to multiple research projects for the planet Mars. The projects include sending a rover in 2018 and sending humans in the 2030s.

Mapping Research

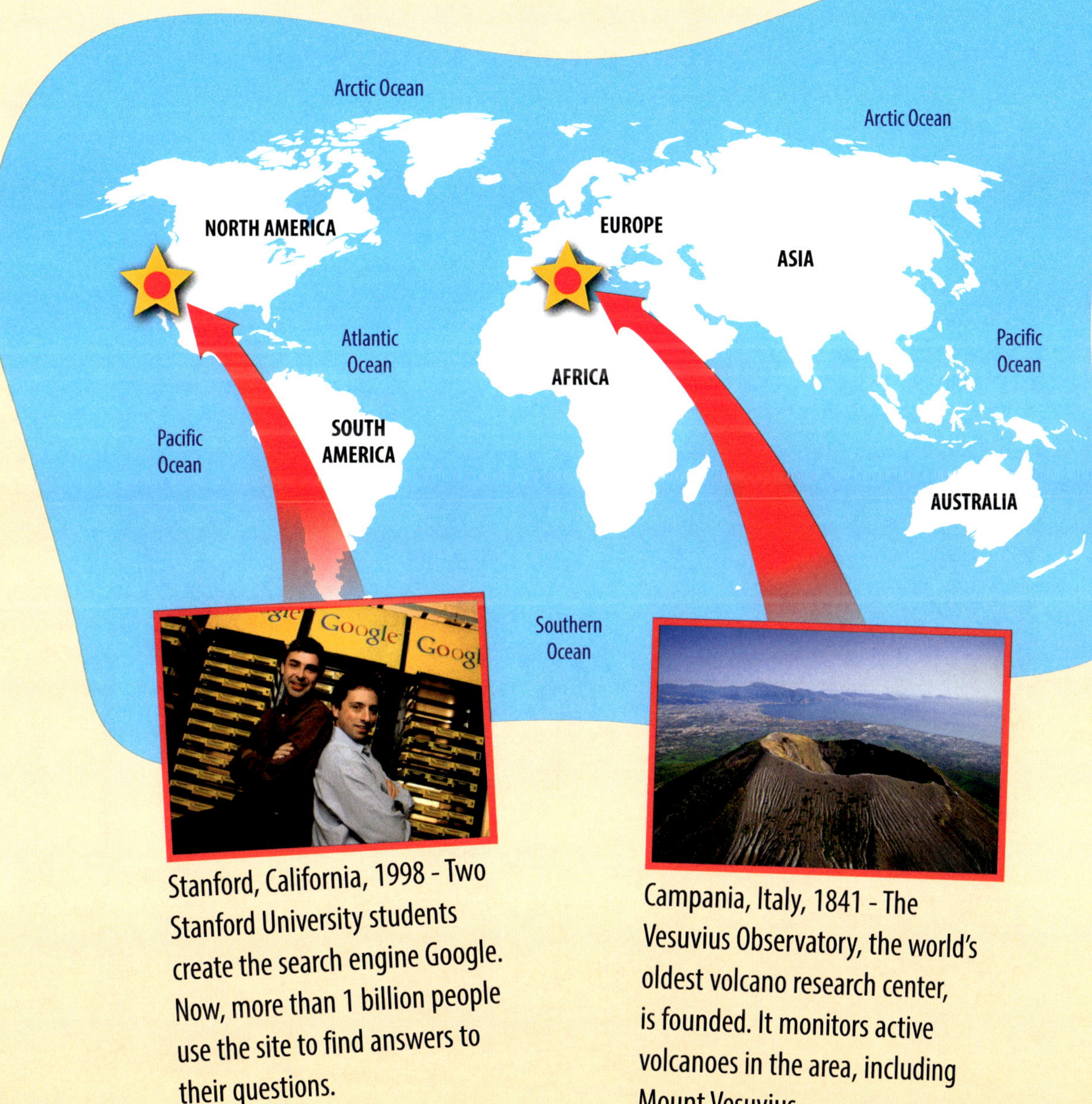

Stanford, California, 1998 - Two Stanford University students create the search engine Google. Now, more than 1 billion people use the site to find answers to their questions.

Campania, Italy, 1841 - The Vesuvius Observatory, the world's oldest volcano research center, is founded. It monitors active volcanoes in the area, including Mount Vesuvius.

2 Chapter Two

Choosing a Topic

Before you choose a research topic and question, you need to know about any **guidelines** you should follow. A guideline is like a rule. Is the research part of a school project? If so, your teacher may give some guidelines about choosing and researching your topic. For example, Mr. Stone gives his students only a few topics to choose from. Mrs. Nelson assigns each of her students a research topic. Mr. Welstein and Ms. Anton give their students a list of facts to find or questions to answer about their topics. Mr. Alvez lets his students choose what they will learn.

Some teachers might have a few guidelines to share with the class.

Mr. Stone's guidelines make it easy for him to help his students find resources.

As another example, Ari decides to do research because a topic interests him. He is more curious about a topic and excited to learn more about it. The research is not part of a class project. There are not any guidelines from a teacher he has to follow. He gets to decide what is important and which questions to answer.

Once you have a general topic, you need to come up with a specific research question. You may want to start by **brainstorming** a list of questions. Brainstorming is writing things down as soon as they pop into your mind. You do not stop to worry about spelling. You do not edit your list as you go. This way, you keep your creativity flowing. When you brainstorm, you may find that the ideas that pop up first are topics that are important to you.

Try This

Set a timer for five minutes. Grab a notebook and pencil. A computer or tablet will also work. Write your research topic at the top of your page. Then start the timer. Use the five minutes to brainstorm questions about your topic. See how many questions you can add to your list in that time. Remember, do not edit your questions while the timer is ticking! You will have plenty of time later to check your list and figure out which questions are best.

3 Chapter Three

Narrowing Down Your Topic

Now that you have some ideas about what interests you, it's time to narrow down your list. When you do this, you decide which question is the best or most important. This can be a challenge. So where do you start?

You should have several good ideas to choose from by now.

Some kinds of information might be found only in books.

Rachel has a list of questions to choose from for a school presentation. To narrow down the list, she first simply crosses off any questions she does not find interesting. After all, it's no fun to research something you're not a little curious about!

Next, Rachel thinks about what resources she would need to research the remaining questions. Are resources available online?

She and her grandfather perform an internet search for each question. They look for kid-friendly sites that will help Rachel find answers. Rachel also checks the library. She asks a librarian what materials are available for her questions. Do they have enough information? The information also needs to be written in a way she can understand.

Finally, Rachel thinks about the **purpose** of her research. A purpose is the reason a person does something. Knowing her purpose helps Rachel decide which question is best. Depending on what the purpose is, different strategies might be more helpful than others. A few possible strategies are listed in the chart below.

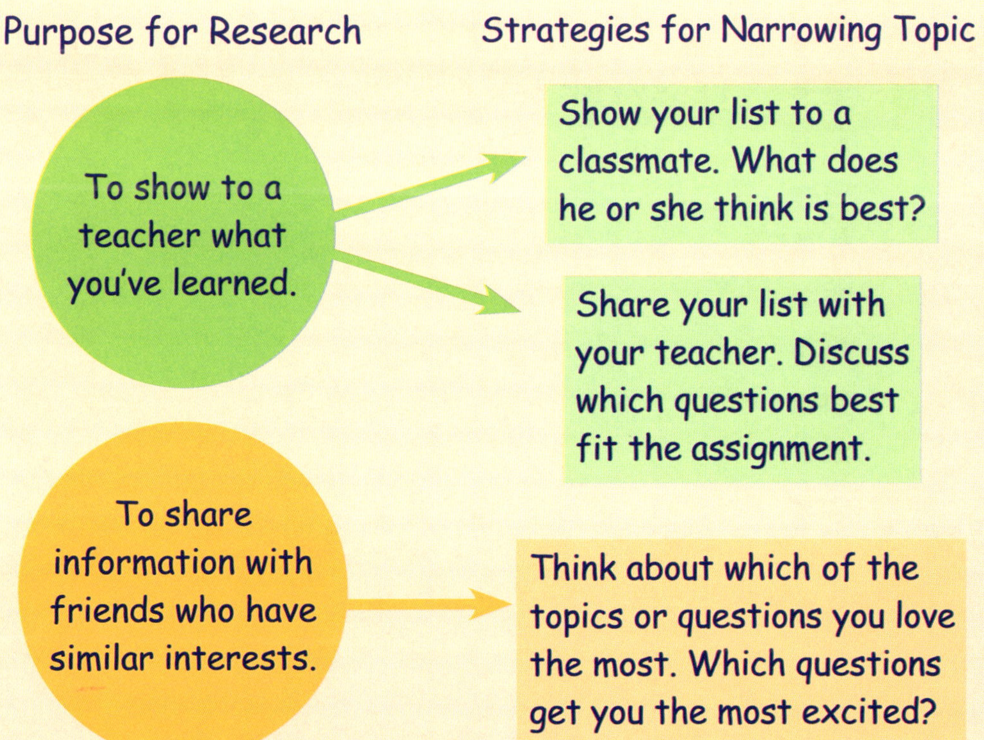

Try This

At the top of a separate piece of paper, write, "The purpose of my research is _______________." Then list any strategies from the chart on page 15 that might help you narrow down your research topic. Try each strategy you listed. Put a star next to the one that helped you most. Now write down which research topic you have chosen in your notebook. Why did you choose that topic?

The purpose of my research is _______________.

1.

2.

3.

4.

5.

4 Chapter Four

Revising Your Question

Now you have a topic and a question to research. Next, you need to make sure you have asked the question in just the right way. You might be thinking, "What?! There is a wrong way to ask a question?"

Adjust your question until you get it just right.

There may not be a wrong way, but there are ways to ask a question that will help you find better information. For example, Carlos asks, "What is the most popular sport in America?" Carlos loves sports. This question interests him very much. However, when Carlos researches this question, he only finds a one-word answer. That does not give him much to write about in his research project. This is what is called a **closed question**. Closed questions give short answers or can be answered with a "yes" or "no."

There are many open questions you could ask about baseball.

When researching, it is best to ask **open questions**. Open questions help you find more detailed information. They can help you find out why something is true. Carlos learns that baseball is the most popular sport in America. How can he ask an open question about his topic? He could ask, "How is baseball different from other sports?" Or he could ask, "How has baseball changed over time?"

Once you have a good, open question that you like, it is time to get to work. You are well on your way to a great research project!

There are more than **6,000** members of the Society for American Baseball Research.

The fastest recorded **baseball pitch** was **105.1 miles per hour** (169 kilometers per hour).

Try This

The chart below has examples of closed questions. Work with a classmate to turn these topics into open questions. Then look at your own research question. Is it closed or open? How can you revise it to find the best possible information?

Closed Questions	Open Questions
Who was the first president of the United States?	
How deep is the ocean?	
Where do lions live?	
What started the Civil War?	

Quiz

1 What is a research topic?

2 What percent of students use the internet for research and schoolwork?

3 What do students combine their research into?

4 How many people use the search engine Google?

5 In what year did Benjamin Franklin do his famous kite-flying experiment?

6 What did computer scientist Tim Berners-Lee invent in 1990?

7 When researching, is it best to use closed questions or open questions?

8 When brainstorming, should you worry about spelling?

9 Do closed questions give short answers or long answers?

10 What was the fastest recorded baseball pitch?

Answers: 1. The subject a person wants to learn about **2.** More than 90 **3.** A paper, presentation, or other project **4.** More than 1 billion **5.** 1725 **6.** The World Wide Web **7.** Open **8.** No **9.** Short answers **10.** 105.1 miles per hour (169 kilometers per hour)

Key Words

brainstorming: coming up with ideas or solutions to a problem

closed question: a question that can be answered with "yes," "no," or another simple piece of information

guidelines: general rules

open questions: questions that require more than a simple answer

purpose: a goal or an aim

resources: things you can go to for help, such as dictionaries or encyclopedias

strategies: clever plans for achieving a goal

Index

LIGHTBOX

SUPPLEMENTARY RESOURCES

Click on the plus icon found in the bottom left corner of each spread to open additional teacher resources.

- Download and print the book's quizzes and activities
- Access curriculum correlations
- Explore additional web applications that enhance the Lightbox experience

LIGHTBOX DIGITAL TITLES
Packed full of integrated media

VIDEOS

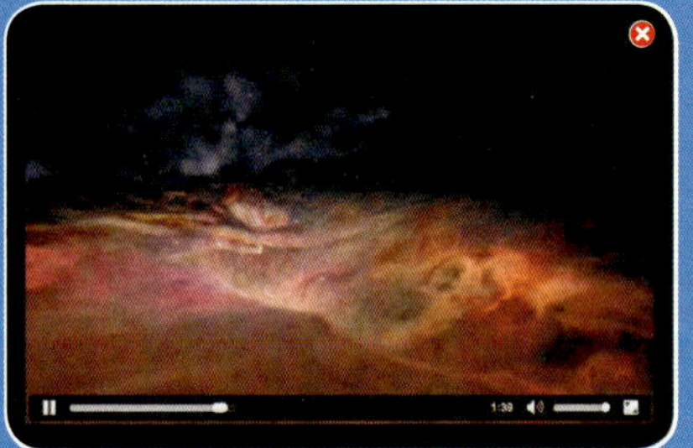

INTERACTIVE MAPS

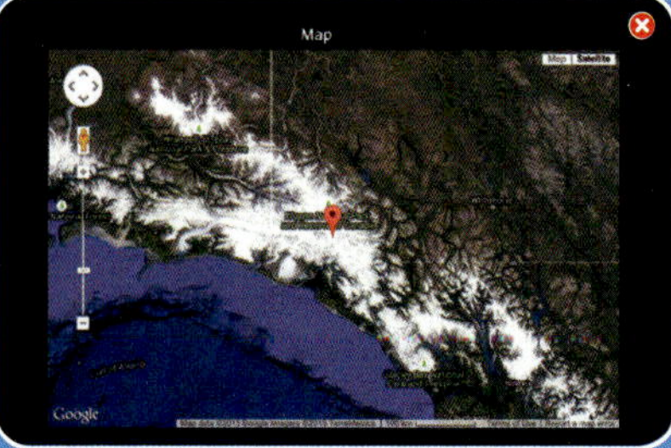

WEBLINKS

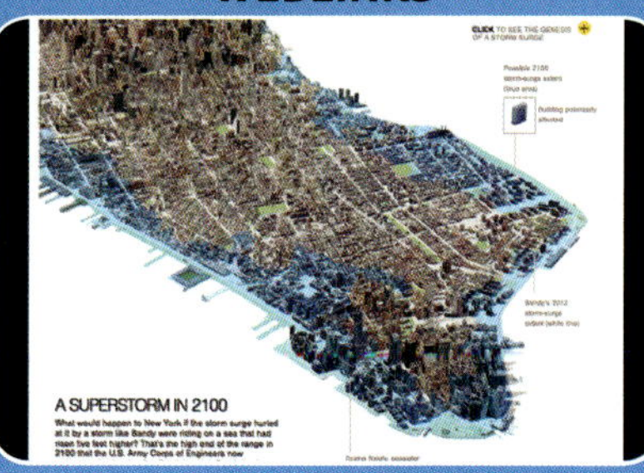

SLIDESHOWS

QUIZZES

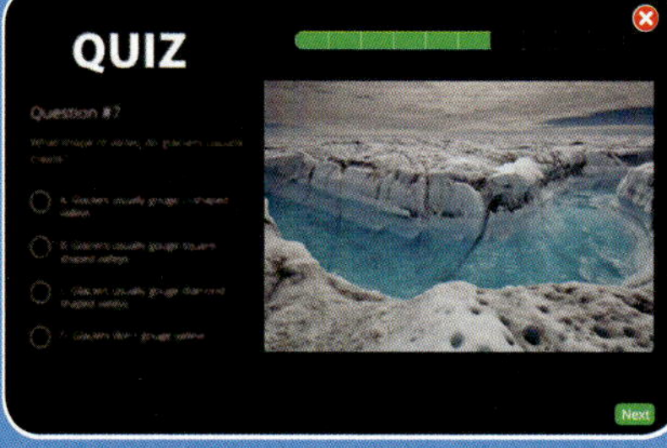

OPTIMIZED FOR
- ✓ TABLETS
- ✓ WHITEBOARDS
- ✓ COMPUTERS
- ✓ AND MUCH MORE!

Published by Smartbook Media Inc. 350 5th Avenue, 59th Floor New York, NY 10118
Website: www.openlightbox.com

First published by Cherry Lake Publishing in 2013

Library of Congress Control Number: 2018941475

ISBN 978-1-5105-3983-9 (hardcover)
ISBN 978-1-5105-3984-6 (multi-user eBook)

Printed in Brainerd, Minnesota, United States
1 2 3 4 5 6 7 8 9 0 22 21 20 19 18

062018
120517

Project Coordinator Heather Kissock
Designer Nick Newton

Photo Credits
Every reasonable effort has been made to trace ownership and to obtain permission to reprint copyright material. The publisher would be pleased to have any errors or omissions brought to its attention so that they may be corrected in subsequent printings.

The publisher acknowledges Getty Images, Shutterstock, and iStock as its primary image suppliers for this title.